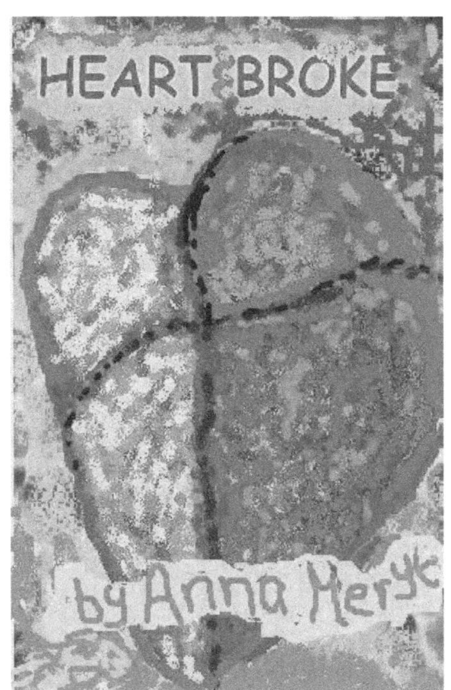

HEART BROKE

by Anna Meryt

Tambourine
Press

LONDON

First published in 2013
by Tambourine Press Ltd
5a Harringay Gdns, London, N8 0SE
This print 2016
by Tambourine Press Ltd

ISBN 978-0-9576122-0-4

Front cover designed by A Meryt / J.Mulligan ©
Illustrations by A. Meryt unless otherwise attributed.

'What becomes of the broken hearted?'
Jimmy Ruffin sang this song in the 70s
about all those people left alone
after a relationship ends
or takes a break....
that's what the poems in this book are about...
if you've ever been there -
read on ....

Intro to Heart Broke

All of the poems in this book were written by me over the last 20 years. Most people have experienced loss or grief due to a relationship ending, no matter how it came about. This collection of poems is for you. All the poems were about the end of whichever relationship I was in at the time. It was always painful and felt like no one could understand or appreciate the pain of it all. It always seemed questionable how I would survive... but somehow I did, I had to.

I hope that if you are going through a relationship ending, you'll find an echo in this collection. Perhaps by reading these poems you'll know you are not alone. Talk to someone else and you'll find they understand – no matter what age they are, they too have experienced loss and sadness.

Heart Broke - Contents

Contents (continued)

The Heart stone

The stone from Brighton beach
 is pale grey against
the blue and silver scarf.

When I pick it up, it weighs
heavy in my hand
fitting snug into my palm.

MerytatenI stroke its sea-smoothed surface,
examine its flat, rounded shape,
the shape of a heart.

A thin white crack crosses it
from between the two peaks
to the point at the bottom.

A second white crack
crosses the first, cutting the heart
into four uneven sections.

Closing my eyes, I stroke its surface
and the cracks disappear.
Open my eyes, they're clear and sharp.

I place the heart-stone
as an offering.

Springfield Park

Perhaps next year in October
I'll go back to the park
and remember how I lay
in the hot-as-summer sun
under the cherry tree, whose leaves
tinged with pale orange
were curling, ready to fall.

Perhaps again I'll look across
the deep moss-green grass to the trees,
the beautiful trees along the tow-path,
reflected darkly
in the wide glossy canal.
There, gliding past as we walked
were swans and Canada geese

and I licked slowly my Cornish strawberry ice-cream,
watching you bite chunks from your chocolate cone.
'Make it last', I said,
'Small licks, make it last'.

Solo traveller

Upon the ocean, a wild day is brewing,
an intake of breathe
starts our solo adventure
and we discover we're alive.

If *you* are there, waiting on the shore,
the demons can't ever drag me down
into the cold watery deep.

And I can bring the boat home
and tell of mad and plunging seas,
escapes from waves as big as houses....

But solo, without you waiting,
crowded thoughts will buck and kick,
corralled, no where to go,
no one to tell.

Tell me of your day -
the smallest details are
the music of our company.

Sharing my day, the who said what
to her or him or me,
I know we chase back
the wild dark seas and
the rhythm of my voice
brings comfort and order
to your voyage.

Mattering is everything,
not just in general
but in particular.

To have a place to harbour,
to anchor our souls,
brings us to the quayside.

Solo we enter, solo we leave
but journey together while we can.

4

Squatters Rights

I was 'do-not-trespass'
but you pushed your way in
I told you time was short
but you haggled for more

I said '*I'll be going soon*'
you stroked me like a child
I warned you this was brief
and you stroked me like a woman

I said '*Let's not talk of love*'
you agreed it was just fun
I thought my heart was ring-fenced
you talked, I should have run.

I said '*I've got plans
that don't include another*'.
you said you'd think of ways
to bind me ever closer.

I said '*No let me go*',
but my struggles grew weaker.
You said you'd staked your claim
and my voice grew feebler

I was *do-not-trespass*
but you set up squatter's rights
I should send in the bailiffs
or slip away one night

The Breaking Storm

A change of light signalled the storm's journey,
all went quiet and violet. The clouds, purple
and charcoal, surged over the hills.

A word was the trigger, not even
 the word itself, the slow calypso
of a voice, in the saying of the word.

'Let go of words', he said,
forgetting to factor in the power of emotion.

As lightening snapped across the lavender sky,
as thunder cracked above the chicken coup,
as drenching rain soaked the olive groves
to the dark blue horizon,
we stood on the terrace and watched.

Later, I saw that the storm foretold
the sound of wailing, rising unbidden
from the caverns below.

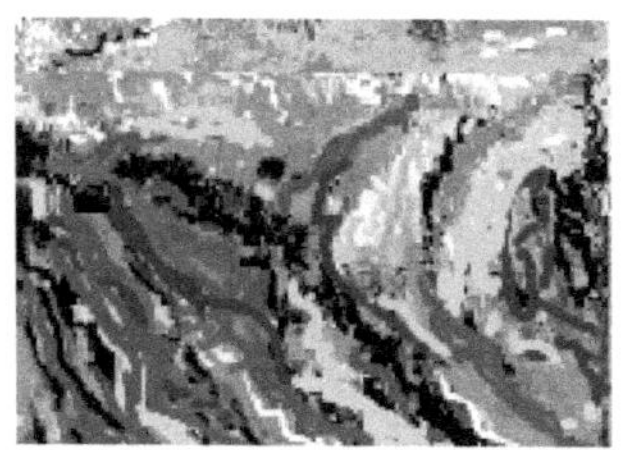

the wall

the Berlin wall between us
appeared on a weekend away
fully formed, shimmering into place
achieving brick solidity within hours of arrival

I hurled myself at it, threw the full force of my energy
against it, pointlessly I pounded, searching for a way
to break through,
emerging bruised and frustrated
by my inability to make
any impression on its rock-like surface.

On the other side you hunched down miserably, out of
sight, in the shadow of the wall, face turned away
set and determined,
focusing hard on the non-existence
of the wall, as if by not seeing
it would not be there.

Sad and angry I walked away
from the wall, counting bruises
and later revealed them to friends.
We discussed the bricks and mortar
until I ran out of talking
and was left alone with you
and the wall.

Hurling bricks

Each time we disagree,
fall out, row
you make me wrong
you make YOU right
then you save them up
all these wrongs
you ever thought I did
in a list
in your head
and when the next row comes
you hurl these bricks
one-by-one
to batter me down
until I sit

in a heap of rubble..

I DIDN'T MISS YOU

I don't miss you, not at all
I couldn't care less
if you don't call

I enjoyed being alone,
read my books,
switched off my phone.

I went out shopping, saw my mates
tidied my garden
planned my fate.

It was soo… peaceful, no more fights
quiet and solitude
all through the night.

I didn't miss you ... three days passed
my phone was on
you rang …at last.

I didn't miss you, I was going to say
then I heard your voice
say 'how was your day?'

And my safe safe heart did a back somersault
and my clear thinking head
came to a halt.

I started to tell you, there and then
that I didn't miss you ...but ...
oh bloody men!

A piece of your heart

You know that piece
of your heart
you gave me and
I promised to take
care of it?
Well its time
to give it back.

Rainbow

You think if I say the words
they will mend the broken rainbow
that these words will heal all,
screen out what went before...

Don't you see it doesn't matter any more?
Words won't put the pieces back together.

Get back, get back, lick your wounds
leave me to limp on
towards the next rainbow.

Staying Alive

You cling to me, drowning,
thinking I am log-like
and will bob you back
to the surface
arrest the slow descent
to the mud-silt bottom.

Your illusional log contrasts
with my reality, where
I drift slowly down
holding tight to any part of you
to keep my carp mouth
just above the surface

gulping air
staying alive

12

Maintain radio silence

Maintain radio silence
maintain radio silence
put up the black out curtains
seal all the gaps
shut up the shop
hide the car
don't answer the phone
run away
far away
and maybe
just maybe
I'll escape
this time ...

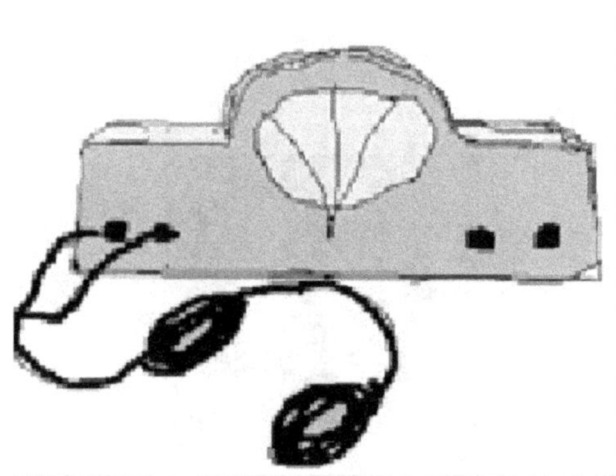

Don't Go

I can't find
the right words
to say 'don't go'
no, no, not now,
not ever
stay, stay,
your beauty catches
all the words in my throat
and nooses them
into silence.

It was never ...

going to work
doomed
from the start

we never
had anything
in common
ever

there was
nothing
we ever
agreed on

except ...

RED KIMONO

I wore my red kimono
while I scrubbed the sink
and as I poured the bleach
I thought of you.

I wore my red kimono
as I scrubbed the hob
with 'Spotless' household cleaner
and wanted you.

I wore my red kimono
as I mopped the kitchen floor
with hot soapy water
and cried for you.

I wore my red kimono
as I wiped every surface
with a clean blue J-cloth
and wept for you.

I wore my red kimono
as I made a cup of tea
looked at my clean kitchen
and thought ' fuck you!'.

Give me a Break

You think you're hiding it from me
you think I can't see it
written on your face
in the slope of your shoulders
in your silences
in the distance growing between us
don't tell me you don't
want me to worry
when that's all I do
whenever I look at you

Is it finished yet?

I keep thinking this is the end,
the last time, no more, it's finished -
I'm angry when I think that,
I tell myself, I can't go on.

I'll make plans,
my rational brain takes charge.
How will I organise my time
now I am one, not two?

Mornings uncluttered,
days busy with projects,
evenings, my own ...

I'll visit old friends here and there
Berlin, Brussels, Bristol
Indonesia, India, Africa.
I'll be free, free.

Stop, stop! Rewind rewind!
What about the empty rooms?
The long quiet days?
Cooking alone on dark winter nights?

What about the daily chit chat
and lack of to and fro?
No more intimate moments,
and laughing together?

And so my mind see saws
up and down, like two old men
in an endless argument, never agreeing.

Heroes and ghosts
 Wish you were here

When I sleep, your ghost
sleeps beside me.
Your ghost sits in that kitchen chair,
smoking and talking
watching me cook and clean.

Today in the shop
I had to back away
from the men's clothes
to avoid your ghost
in every aisle.

And yesterday,
on a morning walk to the park
your ghost flitted through
that copse of young trees
taking photos of me
like the day it snowed.

I want to shout
come back, come back, come back.
But I don't...

Your ghost scoops up the cat
with big brown hands
and strokes her gently.

In your absence
she has retreated
further into sleep
and I wish … I could do the same.

One Last time

Talk to me of feelings
one last time
tell me that you missed me
one last time

Wrap me in your arms
one last time
hold each other close
one last time

Tell me all your plans
one last time
turn your face away
one last time.

Turn my face away
one last time
lest you see my feelings
one last time

Standing in the doorway
one last time
you fix me in your mind
one last time

I watch you from my window
one last time
striding through the gate
the last time

Locked away from you

You sent me a hurricane
whirling me up
and smashing me down.

Now my shredded remnant
drifts along the shore
high and dry on this island
far away from you

You sent me a tsunami
and the waves tumbled and battered me,
hit me with debris as big as fridges
as small as pins and needles.

I'm left amongst the wreckage
lost on this island
locked away from you.

Endings (& clichés)

I'm not good at endings
so when something has
run its natural course and
its *time to call it a day*
say goodbye to all that
and move on, I can't quite
bring myself to the point
of throwing in the towel,
grasping the nettle and
rushing headlong
in to *a new direction.*
I stay *rooted to the spot*
like *a rabbit caught in headlights.*
I *dig in my heels*
bury my *head in the sand.*
But *hope springs eternal*
until one day
while I'm *otherwise engaged*
I find that I have come to
the *end of the road*
reached the pinnacle
and there's *no going back*
so I jump blindly
into change, screaming
'*No-o-o-o-o-o-o-o-o*' as I fall.

How will I tell it?

How will I tell it...
the years of trying to fit you
where you didn't belong
in my life

How will I tell it?
How hard you worked to fit in
to the unwritten rulebook
of my life.

How will I tell it?
But you kept me from
your other life,
a dual life, in a parallel universe.

They will try to make me
blame you
for smashing the mirror
in the end.

Because finally
you couldn't do it,
fit your last few pieces
into the complex jigsaw
of my life.

Walking on ice

I'm walking on ice, thin, brittle,
sliding one foot forward,
then another, then another.
My legs tremble,
the ice crackles and squeaks.

I put out my balancing arms,
step one, two, three,
and look across,
holding steady.

But the other side
is hazy and blurred.
It must be the mist …
in my eyes.

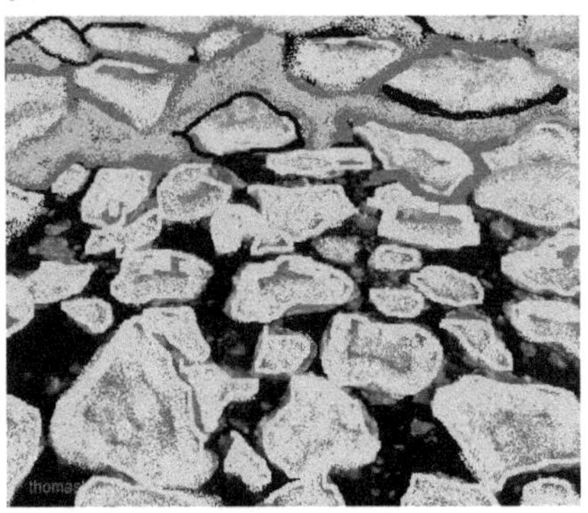

Heart attack

I'm picking out
the shards of glass,
counting. That's the last,
isn't it? No. I find more splinters.
There. It's all done.
I feel a little better.
And then another dart
alerts me …
I start picking again.

A Shell Explodes

In your head a shell explodes
when it's over
and a small piece of shrapnel
flies into the heart
and you curl up in a foetal position
pain radiating through your body
to your fingertips

and you go through the motions
of your life, smiling and talking
as if you were alive
and people think you're ok

but you know that deep down
inside
you're dead.

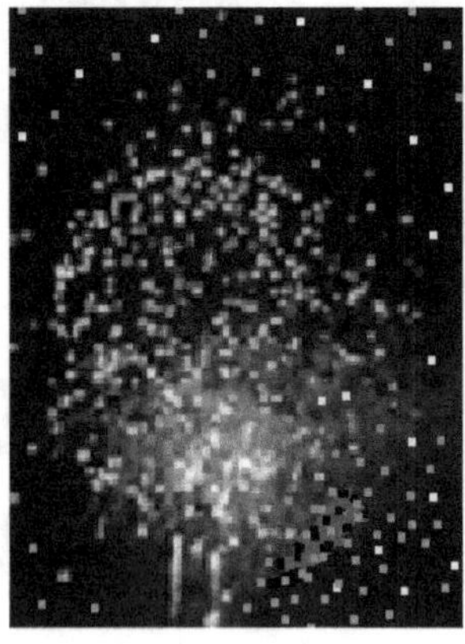

Absence

When you were here
we tended the garden together
digging and planting
in silent harmony.

Now you are gone
I water it,
I snip the dead heads,
I arrange the pots,
so colours harmonise.
I look at it through the window
occasionally…….

But the garden knows,
the garden feels
my absent heart.

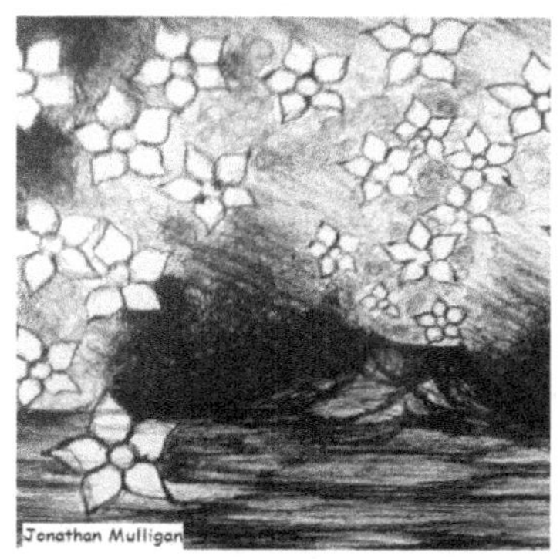

Remembering

Looking at your face
my eyes go into soft focus
your voice is a distant murmur

hearing your voice and
seeing you close
I just want you to kiss me again.

Dreaming of your face
I stop myself from calling you to say,
I need you, please come now.

The memory of your touch
is an empty ache.
I just want you to hold me again.

Remembering your face
when a song you like is played
the pain sharp then fading

into memory …….
blocked out by time and distance.
Do I want to see you again?

Displacement

There are times
when I cannot look
my own grief in the eye.

There are times
when TV, internet, alcohol
are the only medication for the mind.

There are times
when grief and loss are expressed
only through displacement.

At those times
I can cry a deluge
for Princess Diana, Whitney, Mandela ...

At those times
I link to collective grief
break down the party wall ...

After those times
I blow my nose
                    and carry on. . .

....breaking up is hard to do....

Some things can help you get through and carry on.
It's always a work in progress -
* walking, walking, fast walking – in the park, up the street, by the sea, on a Wii.
* Writing it down – poems, letters, just notes – writing brings those deepest feelings out into the the open – just for you, no one else has to see what you wrote. I find that when it's out there, on a piece of paper, written down, I can let go of that one and move on to the next one (see Heart Attack).
* Reading some authors that uplift and inspire - (Google/Bing their books, FB page, Twitter) eg.
   - Esther & Jerry Hicks/Wayne Dwyer
   - Melodie Beattie/ Denise Lynn
   - Carolyne Myss
   - Eckhart Tolle
   - David Mitchie
   - Sangharakshita
   - The Dalai Llama
   - Thich Nhat Hanh

But sometimes positive thinking and affirmation stuff just doesn't work. Sometimes you just want to be miserable and wallow. Sometimes you have no choice – you ARE miserable. Shut yourself away and do it. Avoid people who want to 'cheer you up'. Give yourself some quiet time. But if it lasts too long you may need help. RING SOMEONE..

Author

Anna Meryt has been writing poetry all her life and had her first poem – an anti-war poem – published in her convent school magazine in Wales. She has had *many* single poems published in anthologies, including The West In Her Eye, and Her Mind's Eye (ed. Rachel Lever) (1999), most recent - Highgate Poet's anthology (The Space It Might Take, Aug 2014) and The Book of Love and Loss ed. June Hall, RV Bailey, Oct 2014. Various other poems have been published in a variety of poetry magazines.

She has been a performance poet for many years and is a member of Highgate Poets, a very active poetry group in North London. In 2011 she won first prize in the Lupus International poetry competition for her poem Bulawayo – about her birth place.

She has also completed her first book –
A Hippopotamus at the Table - a memoir set in South Africa in the 1970s, where she lived a long time ago (now on Kindle)…published Oct 2015.

Have a look at her blog : www.ameryt.com

9 780957 612204